Topping The Top

Topping The Top

How to reach the top and be there

"Ability to convert a little spark into a gigantic fire and bask in its glory is no child's play…"

Kallings

PARTRIDGE

A Penguin Random House Company

To order additional copies of this book, contact
Partridge India
000 800 10062 62
orders.india@partridgepublishing.com

www.partridgepublishing.com/india

Contents

Lesson

When you are exploring to do something atypical and out of the box. Hardly anyone will stand by you to support at that juncture, as those paths were never travelled. So you have to tide over extremely difficult times, win important battles all by yourself and walk many a miles alone until you prove them all wrong… and they come back to surround you for a life time again..

I don't mind following the unprecedented path even if it calls for herculean efforts anyways…

That's the difference between a winner and a loser…Kallings…

Purpose

"How is your score line after this years Appraisal? Nothing great?"

Don't worry a lot, instead stay cool, composed and restart again. Running away is not the solution neither is giving up. No body is a born winner or a loser, take heart and a deep breath, for sure your days will come sooner than you can ever predict. Check once how you can soon out class others in no time at all by just using some basic sense and self introspection nothing more.

Folks, this book is aimed at all working professionals who join an organisation with lot of hope, aspiration and expectation. While some meet their desire and excel others just fade away or carry on with the wind often changing path, direction, style of working and still not really knowing where the fruit really is and even worse how to grab them, forget about eating it, of course the right way, irrespective of whether you work in - Customer Support Desk as a Coordinator, in the ever vibrant Sales and Marketing department, Business Development, Production, Technical, HR, IT, Legal, Production, Dispatch, R&D, Finance or anywhere else in the organisation. Actually it has nothing to do with your scope of work that you perform.

Topping the Top aims at many aspects which you rarely hear about but if you know them well in advance it always helps you to push ahead of your pals. Ultimately though, even after knowing these unusual things, you still need to walk that extra mile or two in order to achieve your desired goals. *Attitude – a Positive One* - more than makes up and that's the only difference between a successful person and not so successful one – purely on professional grounds only.

The *Will 2 Win* is a good quality to have but with constant failure sometimes it puts you in a tough corner and that very desire which was so close to your heart not so long ago starts to diminish rapidly and compels you to surrender meekly to the surroundings or the environment you belong. You just start flowing with the wave much to your dislike and long before you discern you are already engulfed in that storm, however strongly you resist now, time will no more be on your side to take you to any greener pastures sooner.

Friends!! Wake up, avoid those circumstances intelligently so that you are always in a position of envy and not otherwise… To achieve this once, may not be a problem but to continuously keep doing it successfully over a period of your professional career is very unlikely to say the least, unless you really sharpen your skills and ever ready to work on your reflexes so that they remain as sharp as a razor every time you call for its service.

Come, let's see how we can come close to these desire of ours without having to reinvent anything at all… Just simple common sense can keep you above the pack, if you are ready to accept the reality and work in accordance.

This professional high intensity book is just an eye opener for all those who want to be successful in their professional career or be better at-least than otherwise one would be and not just count the hour sitting in your desk with a sharp eye on the clock.

Surely we will soon start realising that you are suddenly doing much better and ahead of the rest always in whatever you are engaging yourself into. This automatic visible transformation will help to keep you in a very high self esteem and definitely ensure your entire professional life is much smoother in days to come. The positive energy and vive that will generate around you now shall definitely inspire others in the vicinity as well. So as a bonus you will broaden your horizon with a basket full of friends as well if I am permitted to call them so unwillingly though... be aware not to keep them all in your wallet instantly.

Again, most importantly don't be over duly worried at any point of time about what you did not achieve till now but that batch mate or colleague of yours has, this just puts your down unnecessarily by many a notches without any value addition really.

After all this is no *"Football Match"* we are playing that you need to fix the score line in 90 minutes sharp, come what may. Rather it's a very long and sometimes boring game with no time limit at all and the sooner you realise it the better your ultimate end results will be.

Always remember it's a journey you are undertaking and the destiny is not known to anyone except you. Sounds absurd... Not at all friends!! As you build your strengths, acquire more knowledge, gain experience, modify yourself as a person and sharpen your skills daily, you start to reap the benefits and move towards your "Target Destiny." Again, this Target Destiny should be the buzz word in your life as you align yourself to it and then the rest is just round the corner, that's for sure. **So why wait!! Let's get cracking!!!**

For all my well wishers, Parents and those fantastic colleagues and superiors of mine, I had the opportunity to work with, in this wonderful and highly enriching professional journey- which still continues.

Also a part of the earning from this book will go towards

"Higher studies of Girl child"

Irrespective of colour, race, region or
social stature in times to come...

Let bygones not be bygones

One fine morning as I start introspecting deep inside into my professional career, scribbling the events gone by and the innumerable incidents which can shape or break a person's future, I soon realise that there lies a trick or two which I missed way back then or ignored all together as I was not matured enough to take advantage of that situation. Truly, I lost then and discerned much later that winning and losing are all a part of the game, we exist to play but what eventually matters is the leanings we conceive for a life time which should be applied with full gusto to surge ahead and be successful even in the most adverse situations. No looking back this time.

These small happenings were hardly perceived and often neglected then but now it has finally convinced me that yes if these were understood and taken care of way back, life could have been even better and more purposeful. Every minutest of things that happens in our surroundings must be scientifically scrutinised and well understood so that we are not caught off guard for lack of understanding.

As we continue with our daily routine job and mostly engage ourselves in firefighting of sorts just to keep the flame away from us, we miss many finer points and never ponder about the chances which braced us and went a begging in between but unfortunately we could never take advantage of that as we either- never realised the under current, were too ignorant or did not want the grind which was associated. Sheer foolishness this. In today's corporate world we should not restrict ourselves to only our arena but given the first opportunity – *"Widen our horizon and accept the challenges."*

Never the less as life is becoming still more challenging, dynamic and to say the least turbulent, we need to also understand every minor points from day one to not only reach the top but to stay there as well. There was a time when reaching the top or going up the corporate ladder was difficult and enduring but once there, it was relatively easy to keep your place cemented. Today reaching the top or even gain some height in corporate hierarchy is as difficult as being there even for some time and run the show to perfection under plenty of watchful eyes. There is no dearth of qualified and experienced people hounding on the same position and wants to be there *"by hook or by crook."* It is that *crook* which we also need to understand before even dreaming to reach that destiny some day.

Today recession hits every other year which were previously happening only in decades and so fast is the erosion that Chennai (India) produces more cars than Detroit (USA) – can you believe, where population has sunk by almost 50 percent today which was more than a million just a decade ago. No more we can ignore staying in Europe what's happening in Asia and similarly even if Greek's economy collapses Brazil may also be in the firing line and get badly hit. So vastly globalised we have become that a simple cash crunch in one European Bank may hit you strongly even if you are working in Nairobi (Kenya), within days. A Little upward oil index movement in Saudi can bring your share market crashing down where ever you are in the world in a matter of few hours, believe you me.

So, the need of the hour is to prepare yourself and think that you are a *"Global Citizen"* and keep yourself apprised of the entire happenings in your surroundings and much beyond not only in your domain but also to the extent possible in other domains as well. Get that right immediately time is precious and not on your side anymore.

Having worked with a few reputed MNCs for a long time I feel that each organisation has a complete different working style and atmosphere but the *Brass Jacks* remains the same but spelt differently only. Every institute wants to be profitable and expand irrespective of their style of management and work process they follow. One may be very *Process oriented, others - Copy Book, Safety conscious, Aggressive, Conservative, Speculative, Imaginative, Practical, Opportunist or None at all* but all would have a common desire- to achieve a constant growth in *"Top and bottom line"* for sure as stagnation is as good as – *"Fate written all over the wall."* At times priority and the time line to achieve the required results may differ from one business to another depending upon organisational need and the local environment in which they operate in but once you understand these basics very early in your professional journey and retain these thoughts within, you are up to it. Take this very seriously in case your department or unit is not making rapid strides towards those desired top and bottom lines within the given time frame you will soon meet with irreversible erosion of that precious working capital and ultimately meet your fate which is not rosy at all. It doesn't really matter whether you are the senior most people in the company or just joined as a trainee a few weeks back. I have often met many junior colleagues totally ignorant about this and at times not even ready to accept responsibility and accountability with the simple pretext that it either doesn't fall in my horizon or I am too junior to be impacted, so "I don't really bother" – they say. How wrong the thought process is you will soon understand, and if you carry forward this attitude very quickly you will be regarded as not a team player at all. Avoid this even if you are reluctant to be totally involved in the cause, at least be a part and remain an active listener. Always show that you are ever willing to extend your arms even if it is not in your KRA per se. Time will tell that you are in the right direction then and investing really wisely even in your early days, so returns will not only be sweet with time but also be much bigger and better than all those who remained ignorant to the cause for sure. Know one more important fact here – you are also just opening the flood gates for future slowly, and believe me others who matters are watching closely.

As you slowly intend to make a paradigm change in your attitude relax and take your time to slowly sink into this idea first and never rush with full throttle as then you may run out of fuel soon.

Learning's...

Quickly get into the grove while you are still young and new. Adaptability and acceptability will hold the key here. The better you buy in the ideas the quicker you excel ...

Limiting your limitations

Early on in your professional life and if possible throughout your long journey for that coveted march towards your *"Target Destiny"* keep yourself out of any restrictions to the extent possible with respect to location preference, scope of work, departmental affinity etc unless and until you are sure that it is not your cup of tea and your skill set just won't permit you to do well there. Sometimes unknown - territories, people, setup, environment and surrounding bring the best out of a person which so easily would have been missed out by the predecessor who was working in the same environment before. Of course you can always opt for the better option whenever they are available and if you are really sure. Remember getting something from the organisation naturally is vastly different from getting something on request or by applying pressure.

"A crying baby gets the milk" is not a bad strategy but it lasts till the mother has the milk in her to provide, thereafter be strong enough to choose your milk from elsewhere -- universal truth remains – we all will definitely need the milk to survive, keep that close to your heart and chose your line of action accordingly.

Very early in my profession I was working with one of the Engineering Giants in India, in Sales and Marketing division. Three of us joined the organisation together in the same level at the same time. By virtue of my performance in the initial enduring basic training program I was given an option to choose my territory from the vacant list that was available. Instantly I chose Jamshedpur (India) – Where the *Tata Steel* belongs knowing the potential of the place, business environment and the facilities available there. Key point here is I was given the choice and I did not ask for it. It was really a good decision, at that initial stage of my carrier since I learned so much and kept on excelling in my job with some very good rewards. More than three years later, I was given a promotion and moved out of Jamshedpur. One of my colleagues who also joined with me at the same time was doing reasonably well in his territory elsewhere kept on telling the management that, had he been given my territory he would have done much better than me as the place is full of potential. Now his chance came and he insisted to get the location I just vacated, which he eventually succeeded in getting. His performance after a year in that territory was miserable and had to look out of the organisation for a greener pasture in less than a year since. Why did it happen to a person who was doing reasonably well even until recently before he shifted his base?

Think what must have gone wrong then? Firstly you need to gauge yourself smartly, where you actually stand. Here you definitely have to be very frank with yourself. Fact remains, the territory where he worked previously was grossly different from mine in many aspects. His was a remote place, so just having good contacts with the customer base was enough to do reasonably well as there, customers felt enlightened whenever someone came to visit them being in a remote location this is quite a natural phenomenon. Generally they spoke everything else apart from business. That was the requirement there and my friend excelled in that department really well only difference being he did not realise the same himself. Unfortunately in my domain, it was a different ball game all together. Very educated global customers polished in their mannerisms, technically very sound and expected their service provider should also be equally equipped hence their requirements were vastly different. They wanted to know more about the technical aspect of the product and cost benefit analysis to ensure it is the best choice for their application and the organization nothing else, no peep talk were required and all merits had to be shown not only on paper but practically as well sometimes with trials and testimonials. My colleague unfortunately ignored these finer points as he was too busy counting my achievements and not the process and the grinding I had to go through. It was not his forte at all and he met his eventuality actually early. Nothing wrong but the mistake was costly for him as he insisted for the location and was not offered the transfer naturally; there is a vast difference in the two. Of course before leaving he never hesitated to say, I over sold in the territory by a year through my contacts to a great extent hence anyone else would have met with the same fate.

Friends, how can one over sell in a territory and build such contacts over night, where I myself was absolutely new and had a real hard time sharpening my skills everyday to meet customer expectations and high demands much beyond normal levels?

Doesn't matter really, winners hardly look back to take notice of the negative vive others are creating rather they think positive and just surge ahead, so I didn't react at all when my previous boss spilled the bin, much later though. We move on from here and carry forward

Leaning's ...

"Know your limitations; it's only you, who knows yourself the best. Never ever over estimate yourself. Excel but not at the cost of others. Wait until your time comes. Just don't rush simply because someone else is doing better than you now. Remember it's not a Football Match you are playing and your time may be just a while later, be patient to wait until then."

Widen your Horizon

While on your work you are always expected to do certain things and limit yourself mostly in that. This is what is called KRA (Key Result Area) on which you are generally mapped and then evaluated for your performance at the end of the term.

This will highly depend on the individual that how much more he can explore and exploit within these limitations to succeed and continue to learn more than what is actually expected. There is no set theory available to acquire this skill. You need to be sharp, agile and create enough rapport with your surroundings that naturally you get information and can keep picking up the learning's by broadening your horizon and not feel restricted by boundaries and KRA's. You don't need to catch the gossip that circulates around the coffee vending machine for sure. We really need to catch the *zing* thing which often goes unnoticed and you don't get to see these things normally unless you invest your time and intelligence. In any organisation, there will be various teams and departments which are expected to work in tandem and in complete harmony to meet the organisational goals and objectives. Each department however shall have their own priorities and all these objectives of different departments may not always converge at a point, as the nature of work for each department varies in dimension and direction to say the least. If you are in finance you need to stop that invoicing to a customer who has not paid on time and has overdue in his account, for this the responsible sales guy might not achieve his monthly target and may even lose out on his incentive, doesn't really matter, you still need to meet your goals first because that's your priority. So if you are in finance or controlling you should stop that invoicing no matter what unless of course your top bosses over rules it looking at the broader picture.

By going round the departments and making that extra effort to know their set of challenges invariably helps you to understand the environment much better on a broader canvas than if you keep yourself restricted by boundaries. Remember a well informed person is always preferred than others but one should also learn when and where to use this extra information and definitely where not. Once you diligently follow these you are bound to be more confident and surprises in your vicinity can be minimised to a negligible limit. You will be in charge of the prevailing atmosphere you work in and can gear yourself up, much in advance for that sudden shock from any corner. It helps to invest that extra time otherwise you would have wasted doing something not so relevant. It doesn't really matter whether you like each event that's happening around you or not and also you may not gel well with all the colleagues around you. The key focus should be to collect that information in a smart way and keep you apprised of the happenings to the maximum extent possible. Your likes and dislikes should be kept far away in this context. It's not about forming an opinion or two that will matter but just to know the facts as they remain, is of limitless importance.

Once you start to explore you slowly become more acceptable in other departments as well and this universal acceptance may play a mighty important role in your career at a later date which today you can't even imagine. *The solid bricks you are carefully laying today may return you a fantastic mansion sooner than later.*

Remember one important thing, in your profession at times we just get too worked up and show that expression to the outside world at the slightest provocation. Hide it and ensure that your shock absorbers are better equipped to handle them whenever necessary. Public show of emotions is a strict no, especially when you are consciously working on broadening your horizon. This is simply because previously only a bunch of people knew you well so your horizon was much limited and the damage then would have been much lesser as well but now you are already starting to make yourself visible on a broader canvas so you need to be that extra careful as well.

With every action you perform now you need to also tune yourself up accordingly so as to get the maximum benefit out of these actions you performed with precision and not otherwise, hence this caution.

We move on with the learning...

"Ensure that you are also visible on a much broader canvas and out of your domain with a knowledge of when to use information and when not. Never show your emotions in public..."

Look for the unusual

With time you should be in a position to identify and notice that unusual thing that's cropping up in your vicinity. That extra spark needs to be understood well in advance for you not only to survive but also to come out a winner in case something unusual is really building up somewhere. Often decisions are made in board rooms and it circulates somewhat around some individual in head office but it is hardly known to people in other locations. This is where you need to step up yourself and be intelligent enough to gather that special information so that you are never caught off guard. Don't believe in Gossips though and flow with the wind unless you are absolutely sure. Mass doesn't matter here but the facts do? In today's management style once a decision is taken implementation hardly takes any time with faster mode of communication available everywhere. So calling a video conference with other locations is just a matter of minutes and then you realise it is already too late for you to react.

This unusual thing may not always sound negative to the ears it's just the matter of gathering the correct information to the extent possible well before it becomes an official news. Be careful to understand the rumors and ignore them totally.

Here is a practical scenario which will open up the subject to you. Decade back one of my friend was operating from the head office of a MNC. Work was challenging and he was enjoying the content. As it always happens in such dynamic organisations his

CFO suddenly got transferred to another country in same level. The guy next to him was a General Manager Finance who was equally good and was sure to succeed him. Fate had other things written for him though. In-spite of sitting in the next chamber from the CFO he had no clue about this and actually resigned two weeks before this incident and the same got approved from management after much deliberation. The reason for his resignation – he was a very deserving and ambitious guy but not sure when he could become a CFO here and was getting frustrated. Too sad as the very cause for which this guy left the organisation actually brought in a golden opportunity for him but just 14 days later only. This was a very costly mistake for him as he realised and till this day did not forget it.

Now the worst happened for him the guy next to him, who was the Manager Finance, was asked to operate as an acting CFO with immediate effect and later got promoted as a designated CFO in less than a year. In this case if the General Manager Finance was more in command of the scenario in which he was working and was aware of the unusual event due to unfold in a matter of days; it would have really given him the chair he cherished for such a long time. This is an extreme case and my friend saw it happen in front of his own eyes and won't forget in a hurry.

Much later when I reacted with this person to my surprise, I found he was completely in dark while resigning from his position and had no clue that such a thing is cooking and would materialise so early. Had he have know he confirmed he would have never taken the extreme step. He also mentioned that the senior Management did not bring this to his notice either, while accepting his resignation. I don't blame the organisation here as the decisions were being taken in some other country but still feel at his level he should have done much better to have those net working going for sure, otherwise fate may present you with a nasty jerk more often than not.

These things are not taught anywhere it's just that
you have to improve your smelling grains.

Many times people think that being too curious and trying to
know everything in your scrounging may actually distract you
from your main objective or the job in hand. I don't disagree
either but while we have to keep the focus on our main task
there is nothing wrong in trying to understand the happenings
that's cropping up in our vicinity and specially when you are
about to take a major decision. In corporate world many words
are not spoken at the right time but we have to live with certain
indications and your intuition power should be sharp enough
to sail you through. If you are lacking in this department you
need to catch up quickly or you may be left far behind.

Learning's...

"Ensure that all 5 senses sight (vision), hearing (audition), touch (tactition), taste (gustation) and smell (olfaction) of yours are in active mode always so that your 6th sense i.e. perception is kept to minimal use. For that brighter future ahead."

Listen learn and Proceed

In any sphere we work, the environment will always present you with ample opportunities to learn and enrich yourself to the fullest. In a life cycle the total numbers of chances we get are more or less equal for all individual over a span of time but the ability of a person to listen and *grasp the crux* definitely makes that big difference.

Being a good listener is just half the work done but willingness to learn, retain and implement the leanings at the very first given opportunity is what makes the good guy a brilliant one. Nurturing with the ideas and quality to differentiate between a good idea and an extraordinary one, from who so ever it may have originated will eventually pave the way to a glittering tomorrow.

While in daily routine work you will come across so many ideas and listen to many presentations. Some of these may be just routine work highlighting the present scenario and playing with just numbers to make an impact. These are important for that instant and may not be required for a long term vision. In between of course not necessarily always in a formal meeting but may be anywhere in your vicinity you will definitely come across some ideas which might immediately generate a spark in you but *"ability to convert that little spark into a gigantic fire and bask in its glory is no child's play. This is what will surely make that extra ordinary difference in many years to come"*

We all dream to be there someday and eventually some of us will make the cut too, not very often though. Making the impression should be our last priority but looking for an opportunity that will make a substantial difference in either the way we are thinking today or the process we are following will surely make a vast impact on our future and if you are in the scheme of things nothing else really matters.

The mental alertness and that burning desire to be sharp every single day you are physically present in your office is a tough task as often we get diverted and distracted with minor issues and routine fire fighting which can't be avoided practically. Still we should keep telling our self to be alert and agile as operating in standby mode when half the things easily go unnoticed in our surrounding is not a desired scenario if you intend to scale greater heights. It is patience and remaining alert throughout your long journey to the extent possible will make the difference between you and your other deserving colleagues when it comes to achieving the desired results in an efficient and time bound manner.

Many times we fail to express our views at the right moment even when we have the best idea. We wait and eventually leave the platform for others to make that vital first impression and regret a lot there after. Never be afraid of the outcome because if you don't spell out and express yourself at the right moment no amount of knowledge that you may have acquired will help you make the difference and excel thereafter. If you share your ideas, at worst it may not be chosen and that's the maximum you lose but on the contrary just imagine if your idea clicks and is accepted it's you who gets the desired uplift and nobody else.

Participation in a meeting is always important specially if this is a decision making time. Never be a mere spectator and increase the number in the board room. Be well prepared to make contributions which will help to decide the outcome. That is called contribution for the cause and as you continue to acquire more and more knowledge in the subject and participate actively in a meeting your contribution quotient will start to go up so will be your market value. This is always directly proportional to result and soon you will realise the importance as people will start looking at you for more solutions especially in a difficult situation. This is the desired stage where everyone longs to reach but only a few succeed to be there.

The ability of a person to foresee future accurately and judge the correct solution from a number of options available in hand more often than once or twice – is the key quality of a top grade Manager.

This unfortunately does not come with blood or the gene – this comes from experience and willingness to understand and consider the key factors which will eventually make the vital difference in any critical decision making scenario.

So while you listen, learn and proceed it is of utmost importance to start making those contributions as well which will with time take you smoothly to your ultimate destiny.

Learning's...

Participation without contribution is as good as being absent ...

Sharpen your strengths

While it is customary for you to know your actual strengths as this is also a common question in any interview you will be facing and even otherwise. Over a period of time these strengths keep on changing, leaving of course may be a very few with you which are integral part of your character and personality. It is highly advisable not only to identify your real strengths at the earliest but also to hone them on a regular basis to keep them with you, razor sharp and in perfect condition. Waste very little time on trying to improve your *"chink in armor"* just manage them well in public as it is not only a nightmare to achieve deserving results here but also it takes heavy toll of time with very little improvement to benefit from. It is only because your heart just stops listening to your mind and so the improvements are slower than expected. No harm to identify your weak areas as well which helps you to keep them guarded safely.

Your strengths always may not be precisely about the assignment you are handling but at least it should be work related which could be anything where you just stand out from others that's called strengths. Being punctual and hard working are not the strengths I am referring to here - these are more of your qualities which you inculcated and tuned your nervous system towards it. Your Strengths should be such, where you will come out a winner mostly when the same is put to test with others more often than not. These inherited qualities that you have may sometimes be difficult to identify initially but once done you will realise how easily you can excel in them leaving rest of the pack way behind and most importantly these cannot be easily emulated by others quickly which will really help you portray yourself in a more deserving fashion.

Two decades back it was - I was working with an Indian Engineering giant as an executive in sales department. The venue was Hotel Oberoi Grand Kolkata. It was our yearly sales conference which was going on and after the meet we all were invited for the customary cocktail dinner in the evening. Everything was smooth with all top company dignitaries present for the dinner and chatting there time away with various employees around. Suddenly my boss who was also an organiser for the event went on to the podium and announced my name to present a Cricket commentary in English. I was shocked as some time back he listened to me making a commentary in front of a small gathering in some private place. It was a different ball game all together now with more than 500 people present and not to forget the company top brass. Boy oh boy I said and gathering enough courage I eventually went up the dais and started the commentary which I knew best. For next 5 minutes everyone was spell bound and with a loud applaud I came down to my place not knowing what to do next. That was my strength and I showcased to the best gathering at an appropriate time courtesy my boss. The result was equally appealing and within a short span of time I was sitting in my Boss's chair. Of course all through I maintained a very good performance in my area of work. Certainly that extra zing thing helped me to beat the competition hands down. This is what happens when you know your strengths well and at the right time bring them to your forefront with extreme gusto. I knew this strength of mine and always kept honing the same in front of mirror whenever I got a chance and ultimately it gave its returns. Don't get me wrong -- it was not only the commentary which caught the eyes of others but the self confidence, public speaking ability, the presentation skills and the leadership quality did the trick, but what I actually presented was just a cricket commentary and nothing else.

Similarly everyone has some qualities which stand out and that special quality needs to me identified first by you and then one has to keep on sharpening it. You may not always be lucky to get a boss like mine but still you would get your chance sooner than later to showcase it to the right people at the right time. This will make a huge difference in your ambition for sure. Remember the strengths should be work related to get the maximum benefit. If you are a good singer but work in Finance department it may not help much in your professional career.

An excellent example is about a colleague of mine who is an Engineer but is also an expert in advance Excel and presentation skills. Now whenever you discuss something or assign him a job invariably he will direct it towards his strength and give the output in an impressive manner through an Excel sheet which is his strength. What a great way to not only identify his strength and keep it close to his heart but also to exploit it to the maximum extent possible, on the way reaping rich dividends. This also helps as you start enjoying what you do and that's mighty important as well.

Talk of the town...

"Identify your strengths quickly, relate it to work like situation and keep on honing it until you achieve your desired results. Putting those extra efforts here will be much more beneficial than trying to identify and then improve your weakness for sure."

Don't be labelled for one thing

When you are hired in any organisation they take you on board for certain set of skills which interviewers' think would help them to meet some organisational objectives. Once you get appointed fare enough as you were able to sell your required skills to land up in the job. Then the real grind starts and often one tends to do things repetitively for a long period of time to get labeled as he or she is only good in one set of skill. It sometimes acts as an advantage if you have limited vision for yourself but in case you are ambitious it will definitely go against you. As your arena of work continues to diminish and so will be the promotion and job enhancing future prospects. What does one do then in such a scenario?

Cool, you don't really have to wear your thinking cap to get out of this scenario. While doing your routine job just go round the office to meet colleagues in other department and get the feel of their assignments as well. This helps not only to understand the pulse of things around you but also it opens up your opportunities to say the least. Get yourself voluntarily enrolled for participating in a project that is far from your working skills. This attitude and your ability to grasp things will help you invariably in the longer run. These small steps will go a long way to make you stand out in the crowd and opportunities will keep knocking your doors. The science behind it is so simple, when you give yourself more options the probability which is directly proportional, increases rapidly thereby you have much more chance now to succeed and expand your horizon compared to the earlier state. This often calls for that extra work and may force you to spend a weekend or two in the meeting room but ultimately it all pays off which matters the most in a long career. Also you start acquiring skills which you would never have done otherwise. This makes you more employable and your employability quotient goes up many notches in a short span of time. If you continue this for a longer time you will soon find a new boss for sure with higher scope of work and responsibilities. Again don't expect results too early as you always need to work your way up the ladder and in case you try hard to reach the finish line faster you may crash land. So be sure, gather the necessary knowledge acquire the skills required get the momentum – it's all yours from there on.

So even if you are doing a very monotonous and boring job at whatever level you are always reach out, be open and try to embrace skills which can be easily adopted without much hassles to ensure you are on your toes and learning something new on a regular basis. Don't ever stale yourself just because you don't like that extra effort otherwise possibilities of fizzling out will loom large on you then. We got to be better with each passing day than what we were yesterday and that's the key to success no shortcut here helps. Do not stop learning and enriching yourself however less may be the opportunity but you still have to make headway under all circumstances.

Remember – *"Rusted steel is worth nothing in the market place but a shining one has million buyers waiting just to grab it."*

One important thing to be noted with great caution and understood is that, people mostly have an absolute wrong idea that learning can always happen from the boss or seniors. I beg to differ here very strongly. Actually you may learn from a much junior guy in your department or elsewhere if you can identify the skills and be open to his ideas and respect the person.

I have seen lot of my subordinates come back to me when I tell them to do simple things but in a little different way than what they are used to doing today, simply to change the rhythm and test their adaptability. Majority says I need training if you want me to do this new thing. No harm at all but a few also tells me I know that colleague of mine who is really good at this skill set which you want me to do, so I shall spend little more time with that person to understand this and then come back to you to accept this challenge. The later always succeeds and the former fades away as that training may never happen in their life time so they neither learn the new thing nor accept the fact that it was just a simple action that was required to give the boat a different direction thereby increasing its chances to sail safely and survive.

In a real life situation I asked a female colleague of mine to suddenly make a presentation on the overdue situation of our organisation with some complicated graphs and tables. She never did this before in her lifetime and to start with was absolutely clueless. I helped her to the extent possible and left her at that not forgetting to follow up for the presentation on regular basis as per deadlines. To my surprise a few days later she completed the assignment having done a reasonable job and sent back the presentation to me on time. To top it up I made this a permanent thing for her and was surprised to note that soon with each passing day she was suggesting how to improve further on this presentation and actually did various eye catching improvements in due course. It was a great satisfaction for both and I am sure she will carry this skill in her work life forever to improve her employability. From her side of the story she took the pain to consult another colleague who was better at it and just spent some quality hours to acquire the skills. Simple, but needs an attitude or two – that's what stands out.

Actually once you accept such a challenge, organisation will in due course identify the shortcomings and arrange a much advanced training required for you, you don't have to even ask for it. So don't spoil the show by asking for it much before it is actually required.

Once you are really confident not only about your job but also about your surroundings it makes a lot of difference and the confidence in you grows which definitely shows in everything that you perform.

So guys and gals! Reach out to everyone you feel confident and try to extract whatever little you can to enrich yourself in your professional life. Don't ever hesitate a moment to learn something new and important even from the junior most guy in your vicinity who may not always be your team member.

Sometime by nature we hesitate a lot if we have to learn something from a junior guy in office or one with a much lesser qualification. Think for once you are just trying to grab an opportunity to acquire a skill or two which you are not master off so tune yourself towards that and forget the rest for the time being. End of the day gain if any is all yours so keep that ego in your pocket safely and go out with an open mind to enhance your qualities further leading to much greater things in life.

Carry home…

You are here to learn and excel … it's of little significance – to know who the teacher is and what qualification the person has, once his skill sets for that particular subject is better than yours?

Save your day first

Remember one important thing – you are first answerable for what you have done today and only then come the future project you will be handling. So do not leave any stones unturned which might ruin your day so much that you won't see a better tomorrow at all. This happens in corporate world when you are too ambitious or running too fast than what's actually expected and required.

Never keep the job in hand pending and concentrate on other things which you are not directly responsible for. Often when we work in a particular department requests does come from various corners say from an ex-boss or a senior colleague with whom you may have worked earlier to do something which is not in your domain or KRA. Our intensions and desire sometimes forces us to do that job just to help that person you prefer or to return certain previous favours. Good enough and absolutely nothing wrong in this till you can just keep it to yourself and it doesn't affect your schedule work to a great deal. The moment you start scarifying your core job and try to do something else it might backfire without any information in a little while.

There is a vast difference in any working atmosphere between personal preferences and your job priorities. The sooner you understand these priorities without someone having to tell that, you are on the right track. The moment you become emotional and prioritise your personal preferences over your professional priorities, soon you will be in a dark corner with difficult days to face on your way. This is just an unwanted situation and can easily be avoided with little intelligence. We don't need to say no to anyone in case it embarrasses us thinking of the past but when you are being paid to do something there is just no harm in making others understand the same with reasoning and a polite attitude.

I have practically seen this happen many a times. A colleague of mine was expert in Visual Graphics and making complicated presentation slides. An ex boss of his would always call him to utilise his expertise a lot. This scenario resulted in some irregularities of my colleague's own assignment which were kept pending most of the time. Even a light warning from his present boss didn't improve things a lot. The results were horrible and he got the lowest grade in annual appraisal and thereby did not qualify for any increment that year. This was no ordinary guy but a very good one. True he soon realised his mistake little late though but by shear class made up the loss in coming years which called for enormous efforts which he did put to reestablish himself for sure..

I am sure none of us would prefer to be in such a scenario unnecessarily and regret later. So in work life you at times even need to be a little selfish and always give utmost priority to your **KRA** first before jumping on to help another colleague of yours during office hours, even if *your heart burns – let it burn.*

In professional work atmosphere you are first answerable to what you are assigned to do and rest all comes much later. So the sooner you are in a position to understand your priorities and absolutely gel with this idea it's the best thing that can happen to you and your future.

Do keep excellent relationship with all past and present colleagues, no harm at all. Keep on helping or guiding people again no harm at all but only to a point when you are not sacrificing your work or the quality of output expected from your end and most importantly for which you are actually drawing your salary.

In real work scenario it is almost impossible to avoid work outside your domain sometimes and we all are human being with a natural tendency to help people around us with whom we are close with but point to ponder in professional life is – never do this at the cost of your own work which might not earn you brownie points unless you are ready to invite trouble.

That is – *"never ever trouble the trouble, until trouble starts troubling you."*

Learning's...

Go get your work done first and fast. Ensure top quality output every time you deliver, after this you are a free bird to decide if you want to extend your arms elsewhere as well...

Pushed to the wall — up your tempo

Remember putting your best efforts are no guarantee ever in life to achieve better results rather it's simply increasing the probabilities of achieving better results through these efforts... get this right.

Sometimes you will be in situations which are similar to dead ends with no solutions in hand and you feel like throwing up your arms straight up in utter despair. You could almost visualise that your dreams are just coming crushing down in front of your own eyes and the road ahead looks so complicated that you feel it's beyond you to make any impact and reach the other side safely. Already your calls for help or assistance have either met with ignorance or people are pretending to be too busy to give you that time which really matters a lot at this period in your life.

This is perhaps the best time you will ever come across to put in your best efforts and keep up the tempo even if the results don't show up... Soon the clouds will start to clear and the Sun will shine again but many of us just give up at this juncture and don't try too hard. They just resign to their fate so meekly and meet with that inevitable scenario and embrace failure much earlier than they should have.

Look at this real life story...

A close friend of mine was working in a top MNC at a responsible position. Being a brilliant guy he kept on putting his best efforts but results were not forth coming mostly due to dynamic business environment which was not in his hands. Soon his boss changed and he was transferred to a different location at the beginning of another fresh session. The situation in his new place was even worse with shrinking business and many variables to attend to in case a real turnaround is desired in all practical senses. Worst was still to come when his present boss told him that his rating for the previous year was poor as intimated by his ex boss hence he will not get any increment. He was feeling the pressure already both mentally and professionally but never raised his arms up nor resigned to his fate. Instead he did a magnificent thing for which I still admire him a lot.

On one hand he took up the increment and performance issue to the top most level showing immaculately the things all that he did over the last 12 months and the efforts his team put under his able guidance to meet the desired goals. There was neither a dearth of sincere efforts nor any lack of intension to do the best. He could qualitatively prove to the top management that it was only because of the external scenario that the results could not be achieved and hence he is not the person to be blamed alone. People who matter the most in the organisation bought his idea and his appraisal ratings were changed with full confidence which is a rare case in his work place.

On the other hand he soon realised that efforts alone to do everything at a time may not yield best results so he quickly prioritised the actions and went on to attack the most important ones with precision and courage. Many places he won the battle thereby business which was on a downward curve started to look up within a few months from his arrival and the results were visible for everyone in the vicinity to see. Obviously he won hands down and even his worst enemies appreciated the valiant efforts he put in for this turn around.

The best thing to learn from here is while he took up his personal cause with gusto but at the same time put more efforts to improve the business as well even under adverse situation. As a result of his constructive actions and great attitude he soon made an excellent name in the organisation.

Now this is an extreme case of courage and ability in the most unfavourable situation but the learning's are there for all to realise and retain.

So friends! When you next time pass through a difficult terrain do not hesitate to make the best out of it and if you are made of sterner stuff things will again fall in place and help you to a safer shore earlier than expected...

Don't lose your heart and in fact when you are down and out again in your life – start again with full enthusiasm and know for sure that some lady luck is smiling for you somewhere, just go and grab it and suddenly the sun will start shining again much brighter than ever before in your horizon. It's all a part of our life we exist to live and keep shining...

Learning's...

Right planning and timely execution is the key to success...

Performance Barometer

As we carry on life with routine job our performance barometer keeps showing the results we are achieving on a time bound manner and readings that belong to us very precisely. This measurement is a real yardstick which must be self analysed to ensure if we need to alter anything in our course, behaviour, skills, style of working, attitude towards work and the environment in which we belong to either modify the ratings to our likings for a brighter future or maintain status quo and flow with the wind which we are so used to.

It is never guaranteed that our hard work will always yield the best results both internally (various people who work with us in the organisation) and externally (customers, vendors etc). We have to constantly put our best efforts no matter what and keep a sharp eye on

how we are really perceived by others who really matter the most.

Unless we realise this important trick and ready to acknowledge the same it will be difficult to improve the barometer readings and there by achieve the desired results. Putting our head down and doing our job is a good habit perhaps before your important board examinations but in a professional setup we need to also keep our radar sharp enough to catch those waves which just pass us by. That one important comment from your boss or a colleague just crossing your work station may have so many things written on it for you to introspect, never just let them get out of your attention it will pay you rich dividend if you can really grasp a sharp one and mould yourself accordingly.

Since we are working for someone else the key is to get the pulse of that person for whom we work and accordingly change our direction if required, several times within a given period - of course keeping our genuineness intact.

A feedback is often more important many times during the course of our action to check if we are on right tract and whether we are collecting that all important brownie points on the way. A 360 degree feedback also sometimes helps i.e. asking a trusted subordinate to rate you on several yard sticks to find where you actually stand and may allow a shut door wide open in front of you which otherwise would not have been possible at all.

The below graphs will tell you a few important things, that actually what happens to your readings as you progress in your career life cycle starting from a young age to maturity.

Age Vs Performance Graph – 22-29 years

Normal talent and excellent talent ...

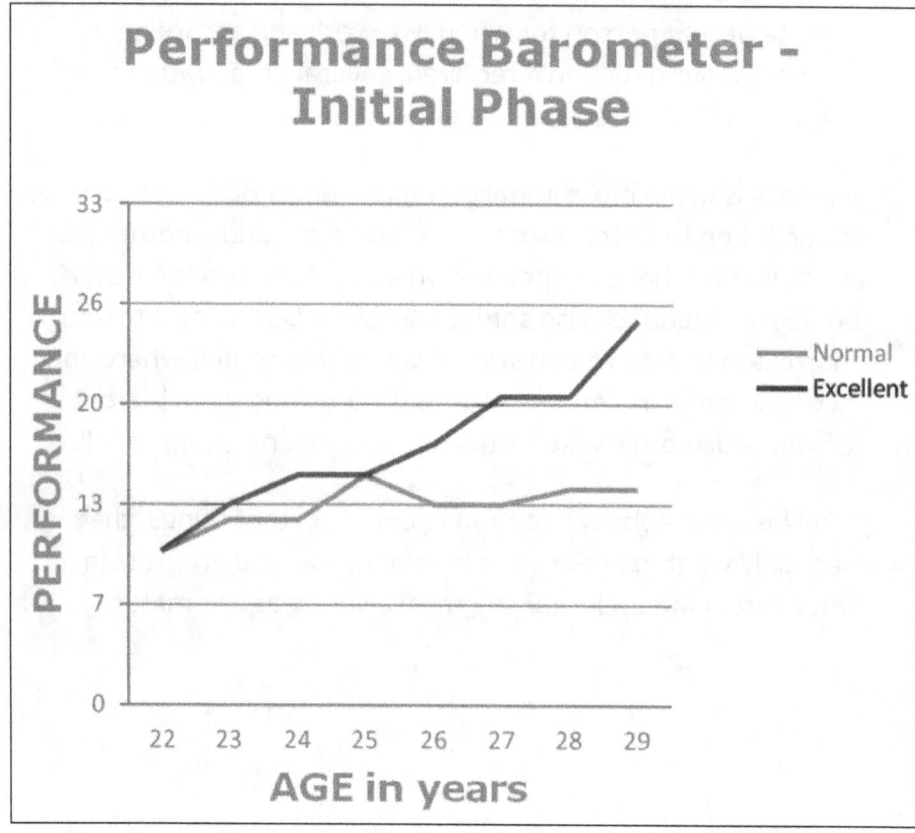

Look at the bottom line (Normal person). This person will progress in his own sweet way initially with little fluctuations in between when the concentration levels tend to drop due to various social factors such as – more socialising, increasing the friend base, romance or marriage on the cards etc. This is a good performer still to have in the team but shall never be a brilliant one for sure.

Now check the line at the top (excellent person). This one is a dream person to have in your team who is absolutely self motivated and career oriented come what may. Soon this person will work towards everything so that the gap with all others in his vicinity is ever widening. On the way gathering important experience, always target oriented and looking at every nook and corner to enhance skills so that he can maintain the top rating and further widen the difference with his colleagues with time who are in the race with him.

Age Vs Performance Graph – 30-36 years

Normal talent and excellent talent ...

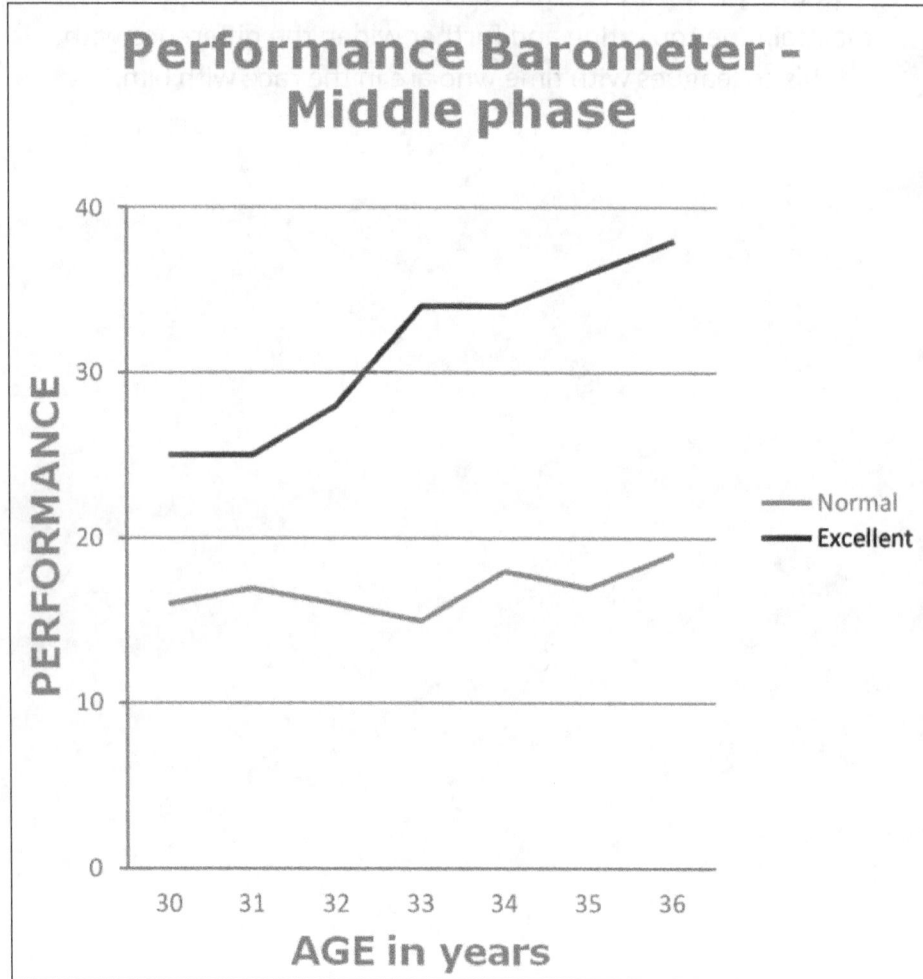

In this graph also there is a similarity while the average person is slowly settling down as he/she may not be that ambitious enough or willing to walk that extra mile even if it means carrier growth, look at the excellent person, he just shoots off and now ready for a big break as he has worked his way up the ladder.

Introspect carefully and in case you are a serious contender and career oriented person never let the opportunities go begging just because you were expected to work that little harder. Time never waits for anyone and you are no exception. Telling a sharp no is sometimes easy but may cost you that target destiny. Get is right for ever.

Chose which curve you want to follow and gear yourself up accordingly...

Take home...

The world around you won't change in any hurry and the way you want unless you make sufficient efforts to change yourself and create a world that you want to own and see... Kallings

Loyalty- a thing of past

My Father retired two decades back from a reputed British MNC at a young age. Throughout his professional career he kept on proudly getting his loyalty bonus from his employer at the end of 15, 20 and 25 years of service. Ridiculous, it really sounds today.

Can you believe I am suppose to get my loyalty bonus from my company at the end of 6 months, one year and two years with the last one tagged to my performance as well. *That's the world we live in...*

Lucky me... I sailed through!!

I got all three of my loyalty bonus by now and still continuing. There are many who actually don't even get one these days as they don't continue even that long in today's scenario, that's life and you need to accept the facts as they are. There is hardly any company who will declare a loyalty bonus after 20 years of service in today's world. This will take some doing. Come on guys, accept it and move on as it is hardly written in any management book neither will it be written in any recent times but if you need to be successful you better store it in your hard disk and not in any erasable storage mode.

An ex colleague of mine who often calls me to discuss many corporate issues since he feels comfortable to confide in me was recently sighting an example of his loyal boss,who is no more given the same respect in board rooms and was complaining but was not able to understand the facts. My innocent colleague could not relate the dynamics and so I told him point blank *"Old is no more Gold"* (old proverb made new) in today's scenario and you better convey this to the person in question as soon as you can so that you can save him or an axe is looming large on him for sure. No matter today how much loyal you are and how much value addition/ contributions you brought to the floor for your organisation in so many years of your dedicated service, the fact remains, the moment someone with lesser salary is ready with half of your competency, you may (I still say may as not all organisation has gone wild) be shown the door or pushed to the wall unexpectedly. The world around us has become so professional and demanding that I am forced to quote the words *"You are as good as your last innings."*

Keep those sentiments if any well apart as no one remembers rather cares to remember what you did yesterday, it really does not matter anymore. Everyone is interested in – *"Have U Dun anything 2 day and what's in it for me"* and better still what more can you do tomorrow? Fool one would be to rest on his past laurels if any and try to highlight the same.

The management fundamentals are very clear now. Hire a guy, train him up quickly and let him start delivering results instantly. Reap the benefits and barring a few extraordinary scenarios don't have to make a long term career plan for the guy. So once he leaves in a couple of years get another guy on board soon at a lesser cost and repeat the process one more time.

I sincerely hope HR guys are listening and may not agree much as they are supposed to have attrition target as well in their KRA. How do they balance this is another real challenge.

This is absolutely true but may not be universal truth as still some institutes exist where they continue to value the old theory. God bless these organisations to continue with the correct breed of people they hired long time ago and still performing like a well oiled machine. Unfortunately today, the world has changed and it mostly needs a smart *Nano chip* to run the machine well. Nothing else really matters.

There are two strategies organisations work on today.

One – a very aggressive company will be continuously on your toes and point out your mistakes immediately to make you realise whether you are actually doing your job in a way it expects. Too many mistakes, warnings and **PIP's** (Performance Improvement Plans) actually hint at your exit plan. If you understand early it is better or anyways you are sure to meet your fate someday sooner.

Two – The second type of organisation which is not so aggressive will ensure you meet a dead end and stagnant yourself to death if you are still there once your shelf life has expired. So the questions to ponder over are –

"how long is your shelf life and can you really enhance the same?"

Check this out later on in this book in *Shelf life.* Learning's...

"If you want an extended run in any company enhance and upgrade your skills on a regular basis. Don't be silly to prove what you did yesterday and waste your time. Instead focus on a brighter tomorrow not necessarily within the organisation always, if the need be. Keep a time check for sure."

Avoid passing the buck

How many times you have heard from your superiors or in your B school that when you are a leader _"Own the responsibility and never pass on the buck"_ also _"never let the pressure get to your team members as their performance may hinder and take a dip."_

Unfortunately these golden rules no more exist in modern corporate world, where there is a beeline to topple you at the drop of a hat and corporate governance has little or insignificant role here. Fortunately still to reach the top in any field and most importantly be there one need not hone these negative skills at all I Swear, rather stick to those golden rules but also be aware of these negative existences so that you can counter them well before these hurricane actually strikes you.

As you go up in corporate ladder, with responsibility in comes uncertainty. This is nothing unusual as you start working on a broader canvas so you will have to deal with a complete gamut often full of surprises and mostly none to guide you at all. _You now need to sail your boat all by yourself come hail or storm!_

"Everyone associated with you knows where to reach and when but hardly anyone can tell you how."

Soon you will have an objective, goal setting and timelines to achieve those goals but unfortunately the path will be grossly unknown and unexplained. People who derive these goals and objectives are your bosses under the watchful eyes of ultimate stake holders and people who derive the path to achieve the goals are no one else but real champions and they are none other than people like you.

Soon the realisation will come that yes one can be the man of the moment if he can derive that path all by himself with or without assistance and sail to the ultimate destiny on time. In case of failure, at that juncture there will be hardly any bosses who will come to your rescue or guide you as the ways and means in most cases are not known to them also. Bitter truth is that if you now have to achieve these goals it will be all by yourself along with the able team at your disposal, so closely work with them. One has to remain calm & composed and remember to grossly improve your shock absorber as well so that it can absorb more and very little gets passed on to the team. You will be a winner if you allow your team to work with freedom under guidance of course but not unduly pressurising them always thinking what will happen if you don't achieve or the sad seven letter word *Failure* engulfs you. It is mostly the efforts which include *intelligent bull work* that generally succeed. If you pick and choose one and don't do the other the probability of failure will be much higher.

After all is done if the results are great give the credit to your team and if it's otherwise own the responsibility yourself. Easier said than done but I have seen both sides of the coin already.

I was once given a huge target in a new territory without even analysing it in practical perspective even once. Worst still, one of the major products to be launched in the market itself was not available for many months so my team's performance was miserable to say the least at the end of the calendar year, no surprise this. During review with management my boss completely raised his hands unexpectedly putting all that was wrong on me. He survived that summer but not until winter that year... Take my word. I still remained for long enough though, to drive my ship to safer shores as I can derive that path myself which he perhaps can't.

The other side... during initial period of my carrier I was asked to take up a territory which was vacant. Since I was very raw I completely lost out on how to achieve my monthly target. At the end of the first month naturally I did much less than what was required but to my surprise during the customary monthly sales meeting it was announced by my boss that I completed more than 100 percent of my target in the very first month. Spell bound I was but didn't react instantly. Later when I asked my boss politely, he told me "I combined previous month's achievement which I didn't show earlier knowing you will be new to the territory and may take time to come to terms." He continued -"doesn't matter, I know you will do your best from now on, first month was a gift from my side to keep you in the right frame of mind and allow you a head start to your long innings."

What a golden start to have and I didn't look back again since that initial month, as it gave me such a great feelings and sense of accomplishment boosting my confidence to an all time high.

Gist ...

When you are in a responsible position your team looks up to you for support and guidance, never ever let them down outside your domain no matter what you do with them while you are in your domain.

People – The prime movers

The moment you get convinced that it's not possible for you alone to accomplish a given task in whatever position you may be but you also need capable people around you to achieve the same. There are ample indications that great days are ahead. Remember rarely you will come across a team member who is self motivated so you need to constantly boost their moral in order to keep them in a perfect state of self believe allowing them to deliver more than what they are expected to do and that too willingly without pushing a lot.

A single motivated person is often worth more than a pack and a motivated team is worth its value in gold.

In such a scenario, simply it makes life much easier for the boss to concentrate more on strategies and other developmental areas and get absolutely out of the daily fire fighting mode doing unimportant repetitive work which doesn't need a quality matured brain and becomes such a waste of time.

Sometime during the run of play one of my friends decided to quit a fortune 500 MNC after working for more than a decade. In last seven years of that in-spite of handing very dynamic assignments and was not really growing in the organisation further after a smooth ascend earlier. After his resignation very promptly and without much fuss he was released. Sending signals to others strongly that nothing wrong has happened. A colleague of his was even quickly promoted to handle the same assignment. Months passed and a senior colleague remarked to his earlier boss with whom my friend had an excellent working relation - *"I think you are not missing your ex colleague,"* referring to him obviously. Truly the things were looking up by then and no reason why would someone miss him in a corporate world where no one is indispensable, whatever assignment you may handle though. I thought; yap I could not digest it though.

Fate had other things written and with in less than a year that guy who replaced my friend was sacked - a rare occurrence in that work place. The simple reason among many others was that he was becoming too **MP** (management Pal) then the liking of other senior colleagues and further delay would have hampered their ambitions in the organisation. The guy in question had no option as he was at that point of time still not up to the mark for this assignment and had no options but to take this route. No offence intended, only this college of him could have saved his lucrative job had he been aware of the growing indifferences that was becoming obvious around him and become more conscious to start playing with in his horizon. It was not to be though.

That's what I always say rise well, rise up but don't rise too fast that eventually will bring your own downfall. If you are not confident enough yet to handle a certain assignment at a given point of time no harm asking for some more time to get prepared before you accept the same in any hurry and ruin your future prospect as well.

It is another story though that in less than two years after he left his position of importance which he was handling for seven good years, had three changes already, trying to find a suitable candidate as a replacement but at that juncture no one showed even a glimpse of remorse to say the least as he left the organisation after so many years of solid achievement and contribution unmatched till then.

Sometimes it may pain you at the core of your heart but its better you leave that alone and march towards a brighter future unless you can put it in black and white someday for the world to see... like I am doing now. Ha ha...

This is for all the bosses...

"You are as good as your team and individually you may worth like footling, so put time and effort to build that team which will eventually drive you towards you cherished dream. Think twice before you decide to part with a champion as the void may be too deep and performance irreversible."

Catch them young watch them grow

While conducting interviews there will always be certain guidelines and some restrictions. In most certainty you may have to work within a preset standard frame and guidelines. Stop, have a look, always go for the best and never compromise on quality here. The new person more than anything else is suppose to shape your future as well so be very careful and get the deserving candidate always who fits the bill even if it means a little fight with that HR head a bit to get that package in order to get the person on board. Do not assume or guess anything here, go for the best available talent which suits your requirement. Never compromise even if it leads to a long wait to get the best match in to your system. We sometimes, do just the reverse. Quickly take interviews and chose one amongst the group thinking that's all we have, even if it doesn't meet our requirement. This is the worst thing to do. You are not only killing yourself but also the organisation on a longer run as the talent pool start to diminish then which lead to many complications in a growing scenario.

Another important fact is if the person you are hiring shall report to you directly or work in your team you need to take the lead and convince others once you make your choice. This sometime may be little difficult but go for it.

I had major fight with my bosses and HR department once to get a guy in who was on a lay off at that juncture. Eventually I won and that guy who went to travel many a miles in the organisation. Having left lucrative jobs not once or twice but thrice in my career without really finalising my next assignment, I actually know it very well what a lay off means and how much importance it carries. You have to challenge yourself at times whether you are doing the right thing or not of course.

Sometimes you also have to give your gut
feeling a chance, not always though.

Another time I recruited an employee at a higher cost from a relatively different field, though I had enough options to recruit someone from the same field. Here I took a long term view and saw that spark and attitude in this person which was missing in all other candidates so I decided to take the risk. My HR did not like it as the package we had to consider was above the budget but still I strongly recommended and went ahead as my gut feeling was, the person will do a fantastic job. I was not disappointed a bit either. This employee started slowly but went on to become a very handy and smart worker showing commitments and attitude much beyond colleagues in same level. In less than a couple of years after induction the employee was even officially rewarded by the company as well for dedicated work and passion. Truly that extra buck did not matter at all in the longer run. Additionally the positive attitude and pleasing mannerism remains always a bonus.

Sometimes we become so rigid and are afraid to work *out of the box* as it always calls for that extra effort but I sincerely suggest to do it when you are absolutely sure only. No matter at what level you have to fight to make things move. Lead from the front no harm if we make a mistake or two. Unless we make a few wrong choices we won't learn what a great choice means - after all.

For all the interviewers ...

"If you are experimenting you may lose but if you don't you will soon be in a place of nowhere. Winning and losing are definitely part of the game; we lose some and win some but if we don't try to do different things probabilities are highly stacked against us - winning even once."

Give people their dues

As you grow up the corporate ladder you also need to coach and mentor people to make them worthy enough to sit in your chair that you will vacate some day in near future. Constantly impart training to your subordinates so that they can benefit from your experience and expertise that you developed over a period of time. If you don't who will? Never be afraid to make someone worthy of your chair as it's only going to help you rise faster and not otherwise.

Whenever people do a good job or even try hard to achieve something special always give a pat at their back and if possible publicly recognising their efforts. This definitely helps the employee to be confident and more assure of himself, which eventually helps better output and a much higher self esteem than ever before. Always be fair with your colleagues not to label anyone or show unnecessary favouritism in professional life if it does not deserve the required action. Go all out if you really have to promote or recognise someone for those extraordinary efforts. Demand and get it if it doesn't come automatically from the management. Remember when you are convinced and asking something for someone else it's much easier than asking the same for yourself. So don't hesitate to take that extra pain to make things happen. No harm if you have to fight a bit more than normal here as it goes on to help organisation and the individual equally on the longer run.

A fantastic story I have now. I had these two colleagues of mine doing very well in their respective assignments. Both were deserving candidates for the next promotion by now and they amply made it clear to me in no uncertain terms. Soon there came up a parallel vacancy in some other location with a possibility to grow quickly in the position as the business grows. One of the two colleagues was also personally very close to me, which sometimes happen when you work for a long time in an organisation. Anyways as I thought he was also more deserving and the assignment had good future prospect to grow, so I offered him the position, in a different location though. He refused sighting his inability to relocate out of his present place of posting due to personal reasons. Now having no other options available I offered the same to the other colleague – he also refused initially but with time and reasoning I could convince him and he actually shifted and got adjusted to his new assignment quickly. In a couple of months it was appraisal time and I recommended both for a promotion to the management because of their past records. In no time both recommendations were rejected by the top management with a reason, that company cannot effort promotions this year as the financial goals have not been achieved. I did not relent and went to my boss who also turned it down as well telling it's too late to do anything and not possible as due dates for the review is already over. I still didn't get convinced enough and wanted to make a last try. So instead of throwing up my arms in despair I took his permission to represent the case to the top management all by myself. He obliged and I appealed again to the management this time providing all the necessary data I could collect to make the case stronger than before. Great! Management gave a good patient hearing and promised me that they will come back after a total review of the scenario. I still was hoping for the best while kept myself prepared for the worst as well. They came back to me this time within a day and with a final non negotiable proposition. "We advise to promote one of your candidates only this year and who to choose for the position is completely your discretion."

Ha ha … it was really a tough one now but as a true professional I went ahead with the decision to promote my colleague who accepted the new assignment in a different location and not the one I was personally close with. I knew the risk I was running here but still I went ahead, what I thought is professionally correct.

In a few weeks time as expected my colleague who was not promoted resigned and wanted to be relieved from his assignment immediately. I did not release him nor forwarded his resignation to HR, instead requested my CEO to speak to him personally and ensure he is retained as the talent was very good for the company. They obliged and today both of them remain in the same organisation handling higher responsibilities as expected. They did not forget to keep a very good relationship with me as well even after I am long gone and still consults me personally whenever there is any professional advice required without any hesitation.

That day if I wouldn't have walked that extra mile surely both of them would be serving some other company by now and it would have been a big loss to the organisation which I realise today. True it can be done, not always though.

Learning's…

"In a professional set up sometimes you have to question yourself and the organisation when the best option is not written in the manual, do get it included no matter how hard you need to peruse, time is always right for this. What a great feeling you have after that - to cherish a lifetime"

Challenge till you are convinced

Often we see ideas being approved just because someone senior has endorsed it or no one else is ready to take the effort and analyse the same. The end results due to this lack of interest in putting the desired impetus may go against the organisation in the longer run. When you discuss a situation in depth about various dimensions it may take a while to implement but many unnoticed things earlier which were ignored now becomes visible which in turn helps us to *plug the gaps*...

It doesn't matter who really floated the idea. If you are in the scheme of things you have every right to question the decision or the floated idea itself till you are convinced. Often while challenging many important aspects open up which went unnoticed earlier. The entire dimension may change as a result of these deliberations which is a highly desirable scenario. This churning of brain or *Brain Storming* is a healthy option to keep everyone on their toes and doesn't allow the brain to idle either.

More than a decade back I was head of Sales and Marketing in Southern India. One Monday morning I was called in for a high level meeting with my CEO and CFO. Agenda was very clear we need to close down all our operations in Bangalore as it was not profitable for a long time. The decision was almost taken and I was called in just to be intimated and incase I have some other ideas.

At that point of time I was just months into my assignment so didn't have much idea or figures to challenge their decision or present any worthy suggestion. Somehow my inner senses told me that Bangalore is one of India's happening cities and growing much faster than the then GDP, so on what basis this decision is being taken. Is there a faulty business model in place or something else, I asked myself? Not having much data I just requested –"it's running for last 5 years with one plant in place, just give me a couple of months to come back with an answer." They agreed instantly and I went deep into the business model doing various analyses to get to the answer and reach a solution.

While introspecting I realised that we were selling much less so costs were not getting covered. Whenever we tried to increase the sale it became worst as we were selling more to dealers at cost minus so the losses were increasing even more. I stopped the existing model and started selling directly on cost plus basis, especially to A-class customers and substantially reduced the sales to the dealers which were not profitable, thereby saving on the commission and arresting loss to a great extent. It worked and slowly we were profitable but now selling much lesser than before. The business was thus saved, not shut and today after a decade I am no more a part of the unit but sales have grown manifolds and profits are zooming from that Bangalore unit which was supposed to be closed a decade back...

I did nothing great I simply challenged the idea I was not convinced about and the results are there to be seen. Not necessarily every time you challenge you will win but even if you can win some it is good enough for the organisation. Here of course, when you challenge and it is accepted the leadership and ownership shifts to you and the ball is absolutely in your court, thus you need to own the entire responsibility as well. So better be ready in advance to put in those extra efforts to make things happen. In case it doesn't work out be humble enough to accept and pass on the baton to someone more deserving. It's still not a defeat for you it's just a situation you thought would be different but didn't work that way how you wanted.

One thing worth mentioning here is that you don't need to challenge every idea that gets floated just because you are not the originator or the idea has not come from one of your team members. If you do this then people may label you as a constant hurdle to pass, so try avoiding that scenario. Do challenge only when you are convinced that you can add substantial value to the proposition and not otherwise ever.

Learning's...

When you are sure that an idea needs refinement or change, do waste little time in setting it the right way. Don't worry if all are not with you at that instant. Fruits from the tree many months later will be only yours as well...

Respect – Subordinates and bosses alike

To earn respect in life you need to reciprocate the same and once you develop this quality people will even start respecting and trusting you much more than ever before which is so vital if you have to make an impact. *Life is always two way traffic and never otherwise so do not ever take a short one way route to stardom it just doesn't work to your advantage on a longer run.*

Subordinates are the key to your success and any asset which can shape or break your ambitions need to be treated with utmost care, delicacy, importance and above all respect. Even the junior most persons in your team have to be given the priority they deserve and perhaps much more if you want them to guide your ship the desired way even when the sea is turbulent. Many times you can win battles without going to the field if you have superior human relationship and proper understanding. Every individual you come across in life is vastly different from the other for sure so never treat them the same way. It doesn't matter he or she is your type or not as you are not here to chose your life partner but ensure you make a mark in the organisation through your work ethics, behaviour and stand out from the crowd. When others don't easily mould to your dice you better change your dice to suit them if it needs to be done and you see purpose and value in that. Rigidity is good when you are absolutely sure that your actions alone can give the desired results and nothing else even worth a look but such a behaviour should be shown sparingly as it may cause a serious tiff with the team members you are working with.

When a team member is in need or seeks your help in professional or personal life you must go all out to reach the person and certainly do everything possible till the person comes to his *comfort zone* again. You will see there after you don't need to put in a word for enhancing his performance ever in your lifetime again. The person will automatically take care of things thereafter all by himself; you just sit back and relax.

Let facts be told - some years back a performing subordinate of mine suddenly fell sick. It was a life threatening disease but curable none the less. He obviously went on a long leave with my permission to undergo the treatment but all was not going well for him so he kept on extending his leave. Months later as his treatment was going on but improvements were not there, I was really worried not only for losing a performing subordinate of mine but a great colleague as well. Mean time I had been receiving routine calls from HR department enquiring about his health and possible date of joining. Suddenly after a few months when I was not in a position still to give a concrete date of his joining back as his health was not improving and doctors were slowly losing hope. Meantime my HR department advised me if we can terminate him and stop reimbursing his medical bills. Time to get furious for me and the very next day rushed to visit him in hospital and seek an appointment with his doctor. I went all out now and forced the doctor to perform the operation which they were delaying for his health conditions. Mincing no words I told them clearly - "Dear doctor – by the time you decide to operate him, he will not be in a position to pay your bills as he will not have the means, so it will anyway not make senses. Since he is not improving for last couple of months, please do something to energise him now and perform the operation on priority immediately instead of delaying the entire process and waiting for some miracle to happen, it won't."

God was kind and the doctor understood my deliberations well. In next one week the operation was performed and rest became history. As the guy jumped out of his hospital bed in less than 10 days from the date of his operation to join us back again fully fit. I still keep a watch on this guy though we no more work in the same organisation but I made a friend for life time thereafter. I realise today that if I hadn't taken that stern step at that instant I would have lost a great colleague and regretted all my life. Today the joy and satisfaction I get when I recall this incident it gives me immense pleasure.

So don't leave people when they need you the most even if you have to take the pain and go out of your comfort zone to make things happen. You will be paid back every penny and much more in days ahead.

Respecting the bosses is another ball game all together. They don't need your *"Yes Sir"* always as a mark of respect. In fact to show your concern and keep bosses happy, you need to complete your assignments on time, reply those mails accurately within the assigned time frame with all minute details and may be a little more last but not the least give them back more than they can ever imagine if it's possible in the first go itself to make that *Lasting Impact* which will last for a life time. Always ask if there is anything else you could do to help further. These attitudes go a long way to help you win both trust and respect of your bosses. Be sincere and always keep a positive frame of mind even in adverse situation. Once you win confidence of your boss it goes a long way and often these gets projected in top management meetings. So don't lose any time to win brownie points whenever possible by keeping things simple yet handling them with great intelligence and utmost care.

Learning's...

Treating subordinate and bosses with equal importance and care will make your surrounding absolutely balanced and the entire unit will run like a well oiled machine...

Accept change and enjoy challenges

Uncertainty at times brings the best out of us and unless you explore this beautiful journey you will never be a complete person in any sense.

Just as our body has a natural tendency to reject any foreign material in it, our mind too does the same initially to put a blockade to any *new ideas* which it foresees, might change our immediate future to start with and the same unfortunately gets visible through our various expressions which eventually forces us to either block the change or just deviate from it.

Not the right way though as it will kill that desire in us to explore and wouldn't help to churn your ideas on a higher platform in near future. Sometimes the thought of not having your family with you or all together trying to do something you have never done before gets the better of us. Remember actually we are doing everyday at least some different things which we never did before but here, since the changes are negligible and thus gets unnoticed even by our unconscious mind so our body doesn't trigger that panic button early.

So many times I have seen once we accept the change and enjoy it, out comes different ideas which really help the individual and organisation alike often achieving the desired results much before the actual time line is reached.

Basically there are four types of changes that happen to an individual in any organisation. First one is a minor change of job description within your domain, this doest really need that special attention as it almost keeps you in the same comfort zone so our resistance is automatically much lesser here.

Second type is the change of department or complete job description but in the same location. In this case it needs a different mind setup, especially in the initial days to get adjusted to the new assignment and be used to the basics. Here also the acceptance after the initial resistance is not of very high degree as you almost remain in the same domain but with may be a different group of colleagues.

The third one is a real change where you get to see a different location and need to adjust yourself according.

The forth and the last one is the toughest - when you decide to change your organisation and prepare to set foot outside your comfort zone which you are so used to for a long time.

The last two can also come combined with the first two with a change in scope of work as well. Our discussion will be for the third and forth options which easily are tougher ones to decide with lot at stake.

Location change is a real change in one's life as you need to first get yourself completely used to the new setup and the environment. Adjustments in the early days are crucial for our success. Any niggle that bogs us down will have adverse effects as not necessarily the new location will always be better than the last one. With proper home work we need to get the advantages of the place and keep reminding yourself the same every single day. Similarly keep forgetting the not so advantageous things as quickly as possible. As your body now starts to generate the positive vibes, in comes that energy and thrust which puts us on road to success. Remember unless you like the place you will never be successful there as your body will start rejecting things and soon you will lose that vital focal point so essential for you to achieve the desired results. Getting used to the surroundings and enjoying your stay holds the key. If you don't like certain things make efforts to either ignore them or better still modify or improve them to your liking if it is possible. Once you settle down fast either alone or with your family and make everyone comfortable to the extent possible the results will start embracing your sooner than later. Don't start with a mental blockade ever in your life as it never helps.

For some time I was staying alone in a beautiful city called *Hyderabad* in early 21st century, which was the country head office of a MNC I was working with. After a couple of enjoyable years there I was transferred to *Chennai* to set up an ambitious business from scratch. Before I left for the new city only thing that people around showered on me was some beautiful adjectives. All that was told to me was it has harsh climate, tough business environment, huge language barrier, typical food and what not, a bag full of negativity and noting else. I knew for sure that I shall have to make the difference as I was going with a promotion and good perks. As I reached my location I soon made my choice, took a beautiful house to live in, shifted my family instantly and made them absolutely comfortable again to the extent possible. My god what a decade I had as my family quickly adjusted and started just loving the place making my job much easier than expected. We quickly got used to the local food and started picking up all the positive things the place had on offer– Its culture, discipline, etiquette, the study environment, heritage, the shopping delights and food joints that suits our taste bud. Business results though took its own time but what a transformation in half a decade when it zoomed 20 times and in a decade take my word more than 100 times from the day I saw the light there in one foggy winter morning. It's of course not all that was done by me but the positive vibes I generated in the initial days bore the fruits and what a blast of time I had for sure. If I would have believed those friends of mine, I should have left the place in a few months from my arrival but I stayed on close to a decade and saw the transformation in front of my eyes with great satisfaction.

Nothing else counts when I see the results long after I am gone, it brings in me the contentment beyond imagination when I look back. Please don't worry as you will meet with the same fate if you dare to defy the general thoughts and can make things happen all by yourself just with little guts and that uncanny desire to excel.

With 13 location changes till date in just over 20 years of service I can take the liberty to tell you these facts.

Last and the toughest one we face are while there is a job switch. It completely takes us out of our comfort zone and puts our skill to maximum test doesn't matter at what level you join.

The natural rejection of a foreign body theory is seen here at its best as your new colleagues initially start ignoring you and doesn't bother to support at all. You need to be cool and agile picking up the smell that pleases the organisation. Don't try to prove yourself too fast as this theory may fail point blank. Keep in mind not to sight an example of your previous organisation too early as it may not be acceptable till you have proved yourself enough. Get on with the job in hand, prioritise your actions and pick up the crux of the things as early as possible. Don't try to hit the jack pot instantly as it may generate negative feelings all around beyond your control. Try and be as flexible as possible and learn to compromise even if it is against your nature.

Once you have spend sufficient time in your new organisation start making your moves slowly and let the world know your arrival nothing wrong in it as you now have to excel and push yourself up the ladder. If you don't find resistance and opposition in your initial days it's of no use as you don't gain that vital experience then. Cool down and never show your attitude till you have made that secure position for yourself and never take a thing for granted in the initial stages at least. In case you show in your initial days a spark of aggression, favouritism, possessiveness, superiority complex or try and play the blame game it will make your journey quite a complex one, which must be avoided at any cost.

Leaning's...

Don't go by words of others till you have visualised the scenario all by yourself. Be ready to exert to the maximum if you are looking to excel and march towards your ultimate destiny with flying colours.

Status Quo-avoid unless intentional

Very often we are engrossed so much into our daily assignments that sometimes all our pending work doesn't get finished on time as desired. While trying our best to cope up with the situation certain things which we feel are not urgent gets piled up in the mail box without any action or future planning. For us, it may not matter much as it is not a burning issue from our perspective. Think of the person who wants this cleared on priority and just because of our non action it is stuck up? Not a desirable scenario but it happens more often than not. This stalemate does hamper progress a lot and delays forth coming actions, as all get stuck up in a series usually.

In a dynamic business scenario never view anything in a unidirectional way or always put forth your perspective to the whole lot. Open up yourself to the broader need of the organisation and act in accordance. It doesn't matter if the action is going to benefit you or not at that instant just take a widespread outlook whenever it is necessary. Never keep things pending intentionally just because you don't find any urgency in the action. In case you need further clarity no harm seeking the explanations before you clear or approve the file but no action or status quo is a dangerous state of affair and may ruin future opportunity for someone else if it is delayed beyond certain reasonable time frame.

It is highly advisable to set time frames for various activities so that the indenter or the initiator actually knows when his respective files will be cleared or approved thereby minimising conflicts to the maximum extent. Once you make these changes and start adjusting yourself to the timeframes you start improving your efficiency and others associated with you also fall in line seeing your punctuality and the regularity with which you make things happen without any reminders. This is an ideal situation and should be maintained to achieve better cohesion amongst the entire team with negligible human interference.

On the other hand there will be certain files,emails and documents which also come up for approval but you feel time is not right to clear these as it may have certain implications either financial or otherwise and need to be delayed. No harm in that at all. Since you have already designed a time frame, adhere to the same norm but this time ask difficult questions instead of clearing or approving, seek further clarity and detailing so that the indenter is not only forced to spend more time in it but also does introspect the basic purpose of his requirement and be sure himself that what he needs is absolutely right and unavoidable. It will be better if the message is understood and the file doesn't come back to you in near future as you desired and even if it does you have all the details to further review and challenge your own initial thought process. In spite of all the details if you still need time to take action absolutely no problem in that. Don't hesitate to pass on the message straight and clear now instead of hitting around the bush. Everyone concerned understands that each requirement or need may not get the nod from an organisation which has many other perspectives to look into.

Maintaining a status quo under such circumstances is completely justified and should be done until the air is absolutely clear or the purpose itself may be dropped all together sometime later to close the chapter for now.

Learning's...

Be time bound in your approach; develop a system around you which supports the same without much human interference. Delay things only when you feel it doesn't have a merit after consciously checking all aspects under a given scenario...

Shelf life – the universal truth

While we are working and too engrossed in our daily fire fighting often we tend to miss those tiny things that matter to us a lot. The dark clouds that are gathering and taking a robust shape far away from us are often ignored but ultimately their concentration will increase one day and a storm without warning may grasp you totally if you are ignorant. Remember however good you may be in your work you will still have a *"Shelf life."*

It will be shear foolishness to be ignorant about this important fact.

To expand this statement further – it is indeed a difficult and very catchy topic especially for the boss. Actually when you work for a few years without developing skills you are actually labelled for that assignment only but the individual unfortunately thinks that he or she is doing a fantastic job and is indispensable in the company. Truth remains, that person may be actually doing a fantastic job (his/her perspective) but in reality it is not always safe though. Why it happens this way is a big question? Once you reach a certain level in the salary bracket in a given position there is actually very little or no further growth available if you continue to do the same assignment, however good you may be at it. Your expectations may go up which is quite natural but you will continue to get a nominal increment year after year and if your boss fights for justice, as he may be very comfortable working with you since you developed some good skills under his very nose and the compatibility with him continues to be great but it doesn't work out at all. Rather he is told point blank to look for a fresh or new replacement if the employee is not happy with the present state of affair. For the organisation an individual does not matter as they are too ignorant and works absolutely mechanically, mostly correlating job description with the salary bracket and that's all. Does it mean end of the road for you? Mostly it is not at all. You need be smart though and pick up the hints at the earliest without much guess work.

I am actually very conscious about this happening and deal this difficult subject well in advance with my subordinates – of course if they are willing to listen to me and accept the fact.

Some years back a subordinate of mine working in a support system came back to me hard on her increment and deservingly so after some very dedicated work. In spite of her absolute flaw less performance her increment did not justify the ratings of her performance at all. Management hinted at the same thing as previously explained. The job description does not any further support better increment as the pick in the salary bracket is fast approaching. It is a very difficult situation indeed for a fair boss, either to explain this complexity to the management or to the hard working individual.

I keep trying though and go out of the way and directly tell the employee to develop / upgrade related skills which will increase their employability quotient and broaden their scope of work in the present job but incase the stalemate still persist I prepare them for the eventuality. Whatever happens after this but still we have to prepare them in such a way so that they will be much more acceptable outside the organisation as well if that is the solution, so be it. The other way of solving this problem is to thoroughly check their skill set and push for a change in assignment in some other department if that has a better compatibility. Basically the employee here has to understand the dynamics and act to the rescue taking the cue much early and actually long before the bell rings. Often the employees in question argue, are very ignorant and fail to understand the boss – that's the reality and the world we live in. No doubt that's where, some very good employees also sometimes misses out badly in the race. Sad but true if you are reluctant to understand this particular thinking of corporate world.

I sincerely suggest everyone in this scenario to be more practical, reasonable and level headed to tide over the situation in a smoother way rather than challenging the authority as it doesn't work out that way at all.

Caution...

"Look for the writings on the wall much before others read that out blatantly for you. Accordingly take evasive action. Even if it means some flinty decisions to enhance your skill set or get out from your comfort zone to work in a new position or environment."

Never show off your power or position

You have attained a certain position in the organisation by virtue of your qualification, skill sets, experience, performance, many other related qualities and of course by the grace of almighty if you believe so. Many people with the same qualities like yours are either much below you or sometimes even be above you, that really should not matter much. Remember the position is only temporary like everything else in this world. The power you enjoy today which is associated with the position is no different either. Once you remember these, you will act normally, gather your thoughts in a positive direction and continue to do your job to the best of your ability trying to reach and exceed the organisational objectives as long as you are there. There is just no need to prove anyone what you are as in most certainty everyone knows and that's why you have reached where you are today. If anyone is not aware or trying to act so it's absolutely his or her own problem, not yours and let me assure you with time they will also fall in line, you just don't need to rush to prove these individuals a point as you have plenty of other priorities to concentrate which will give you much better returns in due course of time.

Many times though you need to take tough decisions based on your position, that's not showing off power rather you are just doing what is best for the organisation and since you are in that important position it's you who is taking the shots- nothing wrong in that at all.

While in my early thirties one day my boss called me to his chamber and handed over a promotion letter which was a sea change from my present assignment then. I was excited and happy when suddenly my boss hugged me passionately and vey boldly told me this -

"As you go out of this room you will hold a position of great importance in this office but the world has not transmuted a bit so you shouldn't either. Don't show off to the outside world. I would appreciate if you walk out from this room the same way you entered knowing absolutely noting what's in store for you until I handed over this letter. My friend, continue to do it for the rest of your career. Your job profile has changed but the person in you should not, that's why you are where you are today and others are not."

I still get drenched and goose bumps when I remember this. How true he was and this incident completely changed my mind from that day and had such a lasting impact that I still find so much value in it. *People should respect you and not the chair, people should honour you not the position* – tough one though as both go hand in hand but that should be the aim and once you achieve that only then actually you deserve both – the chair and the position as well...

The other side of the coin I have seen many time in my life and observed with bitter pain the consequences it actually leads to.

Quite some time ago I had this boss of mine who visited me from head quarters; he was of course a frequent visitor to my location. The hotels were booked as per his earlier entitlement which was not bad – 4 star accommodation. He immediately instructed to upgrade him to a five star hotel as per his eligibility now (he got a recent promotion) – nothing wrong I found in it but it was just an overnight stay with actual time that will be spent in the hotel may not exceed 8 hours so according to me it did not merit this emergency change as heavy cancellations charges were applicable which was known to him. It's just the attitude which sometimes changes overnight with people and I can assure you the chair also changes sometimes rapidly and overnight, as it happened with this person in flat six months to be precise. Don't mistake me and think you have to act below your status, not at all, only caution is don't ever over react in a corporate world specially with your hierarchy and eligibilities as they change with position and time and it can also be a movement not necessarily in north ward direction always. Take life as it comes and while enjoying every moment of your success and the upward movement do also keep in mind there could be a situation where it can also go in reverse direction. Not necessarily always that you have to do something awfully wrong but many times it may happen due to the rapidly changing business environment in which you operate or just the question of sustainability.

Remember always, with position automatically comes the power and change in responsibility. If your concentration is mostly on the assignment on hand, the challenges that you will face in recent times you are on right track, instead of wasting valuable time thinking about your position or the eligibilities which is anyways an automatic pleasant addition.

Immediately upon getting an elevation find out the top five objectives you want to achieve with in a minimal time frame. Choose one or two from that which you are most confident and sure enough to achieve. Then systematically attack them and try to achieve the desired results within the time frame. If you just follow this you have more than made your day if not your year as you are often not expected to do wonders within a short span after your elevation. The impact you bring with these little success shortly after your elevation becomes the buzz word in board room and believe me first impression makes a lot of difference which will definitely sail you through in your long and difficult journey later. While not trying to prove yourself too much at this early juncture after your immediate promotion remember to work harder than ever before in your initial days and months to ensure you grab the things faster and always show that efforts are on towards the company goals and objectives with utmost seriousness.

This is not a lesson but the ultimate thing people want to see in you who have trusted you with the position for sure.

Learning's ...

"Always have the correct frame of mind and set the priorities right immediately after your elevation not to put undue efforts on things of little significance, just ignore all those tiny botheration and put your energy and effort on the colossal goals ahead."

<u>Don't be a parrot</u>

This indeed is my favourite catch line for many years now. I can hardly imagine that people who are associated with me for sometime haven't yet hard these punch line and not received a full briefing and clarity about the subject.

How can you all miss this important one then?

World is moving at a great speed and all of us are improving ourselves on a routine basis to survive and of course surge ahead in life. *Survival of the fittest* still holds well in this human jungle as well. Everyone is trying hard to outsmart or out space you where ever a need arises. So every information we receive is of utmost importance and the same *should not* be registered in a raw form without processing it with due care.

God has gifted us with a natural *CPU (Central Processing Unit)* that's our brain. While utmost care must be taken to ensure that it is not overloaded at any instant but at the same time we must be smart enough not to just see or listen anything and act instantly without giving the CPU enough chance and time to process the information, refine it and make it suitable first before we can even think of accepting the same. Sharing or relaying of this processed information should come much later once we have thoroughly checked its content and now convinced that the key message you want to pass on is really making an impact on all those who will be your receivers – this is true for verbal as well as written communication. Ensure that proper care is also taken to edit and delete the unimportant things before it is available in public domain in any form.

I have often seen people reacting instantly to a customer quarry without even understanding that whether customer has really spoken the facts or not. We seem to be in a great hurry to please the customer or close the deal there by completely missing sometimes the *twists n the turns* and the facts which holds the key, just because we either did not ask relevant questions or not allowed our CPU to process the information with clarity. This is a great opportunity lost for the organisation especially if you are in customer support desk or in sales and marketing meaning, in direct contact with the valuable customer on a regular basis.

If you ever watched a Parrot in your life carefully it actual does the same – that is - it simply repeats the words or sentences you say without ever trying to process the same, true it does not have the processing capability but we have. After all we are human being and have every right to challenge a given statement until we are completely convinced and ready to accept.

During my long journey as a Sales and Marketing head many times I received calls directly from my sales team or CSD (customer support desk) – looking for a solution and as usual instantly to either close a deal somewhere or just to please a demanding customer. When I tried to process these information's for a solution, often I noticed lose links and impractical demands from customer just to put the other person in a defensive mode and achieve a better deal altogether. Good move from customer's perspective definitely. Very often these impractical demands were not challenged and information was passed on to me in a raw form making my life really difficult and almost impossible to reach the correct solution. Initially I used to discuss with the same customer again and find out the actual scenario with lot of tactical probing in a decent manner so that customer is not heart but I get to read his mind and the facts without giving him much clue. Later I realised it's not my job and by doing this I am actually spoon feeding the person responsible who will always look for assistance, soon lose his self confidence and ability to listen, learn and react. So I instantly came up with the *Parrot theory* and took real pain in explaining it all in my vicinity. Really my life ever since has become much easier than it was ever before.

Today people working directly under me or in the department are all expected to listen first patiently, process the information thoroughly and only then release it to me for action if any. There is a marked improvement in two ways if you follow this simple theory – on one hand you become more responsible and start owing the information as you are the one who processed the same and secondly you don't allow others to fool you that quickly which is always a key element if you have to be successful in life.

From a very young age I was taught by my father to try and analyse a difficult situation with a cool brain all by myself and act on it to rectify the same before I even think of calling anyone external for help. This is how we should approach any problem or situation in life before raising our hands and seeking help. Most of time I have seen we can generate a solution ourselves if we are working smartly with an active brain to support us, given of course we have the knowledge and expertise in the subject which goes without saying.

Remember half information is as good as information which is null and void. To be in any practical and difficult situation and still able to extract the correct and relevant information from others, needs some expertise, an alert mind and above all our ability to remain sharp and keep the brain in active mode throughout the conversation. It's not that simple though. You are called in to do two important jobs simultaneously i.e. listening with great care and perfection plus allowing your brain cells to process this information instantly with great accuracy so that you can act upon it without missing out the Zing thing... not even once.

If you can try and do this once you start feeling like a winner no matter whether you actually win that important conversation or not but your inner senses will tell that you got to the crux of the of the thing and facts are all known now to take that correct decision if it calls for. Once a winner always a winner as you go on implementing the theory every time you get into a conversation no matter in what context of life.

The positive effects will now start to appear in front of your very eyes as your ability to read a situation correctly and accurately improves so will be your decision taking abilities in due course of time. This will enhance your self confidence and that's the key to profession stardom.

Take away...

"Process any information from an external source thoroughly and release it only after it has taken a final shape similar to a factory finished product, after proper QC. On the way you will learn a lot which may eventually lead you to a solution if you are looking for one..."

Changing times

During my college days I saw a professor who would never blame his students under any circumstances. Mischievous as we were those days - in one rainy afternoon while we were walking on the side road to our class room suddenly one of the students intentionally came from behind and softly hit my professor's leg with the sole intention of seeing him fall in the pool of mud. As the professor fell down on the mud pool lightly and finally got up, he first embraced that naughty boy and repeatedly asked him where he got heart and if it is serious? I still remember the face of that guy at that instant as he was so embarrassed and shocked that he will never ever in his life do such a mischief again.

Today it is a different story where you need to sail your own boat all by yourself and expecting someone to share the skills and groom you to perfection is expecting perhaps too much. Mostly when you take up a new assignment or job there is no one to guide you through the pool of documents lying unattended in your mail box as the person is mostly long gone before you are there. So very swiftly we see the excitement of promotion, job switch or new assignment vanishes as the hard reality strikes in and it worsens with each passing day as you are held solely responsible for all the misdeeds done by your predecessor and rarely complements come your way for the good work done to resolve these mess.

I often notice in these modern days' colleagues sitting next to each other exchanging mails on important affairs and if the other person takes weeks to reply, so be it but they will never ever discuss things in person to sort out which could have been otherwise done in minutes. That's the current corporate we are proud to tag our self to but it badly hinders' growth and team work today. We have become so formal that everything we want should come to us either in a mail form or in writing to proceed further. When emails were not the form of official communication it was much better as a direct exchange or a phone call use to settle issues very quickly. While it is good to document certain important aspect of business in black and white we should not waste our valuable time writing mails and then waiting till eternity for a reply to settle the issue. Guys get up, go to your colleague personally if need be or call him up at that instant if need arise and settle all such issues without waiting for anyone else to tell you the same. *Time is money and it will continue to be so till eternity.*

Who else but you need to realise this value proposition quickly or prosperity will be at stake both for you and your organisation as well.

While we must take advantage of various developments of modern time to make faster communication and deliver results much quicker than we ever did before keeping in mind always the basics remain unaltered that's you have to deliver the required *"Top & bottom line within a given time frame and that's the key deliverable."*

If we are still not in a position to speed up things even when we have the most modern technologies available with us at every step it is nothing but total waste of resource and valuable time. I have noticed colleagues today directly refusing or sometimes avoiding to share that important knowledge to a new joiner with the simple pretext – no one did it for me when I was new or something else. Remember if you are sharing your knowledge you are just helping someone else to learn the content of the job better and quicker so that you can someday go up the ladder. If you don't do it, still that person will certainly learn with time but you will be left alone by then.

With professional rivalry increasing by leaps and bound these days mostly because of the abundant qualified manpower easily available for a given assignment but still we counter a dearth of real talent still exists showing that passion and will to win quality under any circumstances. A person who is self motivated and doesn't need a push at every instant is still as hard to find as it was long time back as well. So whatever you are doing do it with complete trust, passion and full dedication so that end results are much better than expected. Do not look to take that shorter easier route to fame as it will be a short time gain and not at all sustainable in the longer run.

Asking *"what's in it for me and relating every tiny additional work with money"* is something like a style quotient these days but the fact remains that these are all short lived. You are in your life cycle journey where every small event should not be measured in monetary terms as sooner or later the equation will be adequately balanced and no one generally loses out on the longer run if that *passion and fire* in your belly continues to drive you in right direction still.

Learning's

"Remember — many decades later working dynamism will have a sea change, competition will be much hotter, further developments in office automation may make life easier and you need to adapt to these changes if you are still working. Unfortunately what will never change is - organisations will still look for the Top & Bottom line only - unless you are lucky enough and working for a charitable cause."

Unlearn to learn

Unlike any other equipment or instrument we deal with, the CPU (Central Processing Unit) in our brain has limitless capacity to store and process things simultaneously. The more we keep it sharp and agile the maximum value we can extract out of it all processed to perfection and served in a platter. So our brain storage cells has no limitations at all but it's only our mind which has these limitations as we have in any other devise we use today which clearly states the storage capacities as - MB, GB, TB or PB (TB – Terabyte -1024 GB = 1TB & PB – Petabyte – 1024 TB = 1 PB) and this is a well know fact. All is true up to this juncture but now we have to understand the facts and explore more into this subject.

As we keep learning new things in our daily professional work cycle, sometimes there may be contradiction of ideas with what we learned way back. This is quite a natural phenomenon as the world is changing and new things are being invented to make the older ones many a times look obsolete or even make them redundant. Our ability to excel further will not only depend on how we embrace the new ideas with open arms but also to use the CPU, get the right logic, be convinced and only then accept the new floating idea. Once we are convinced that yep this idea is for keeps, try to unlearn the older version which directly opposes the new one. Our ability and acceptance to delete something permanently from the memory cells is not at all an easy process by any means as it has already been embossed somewhere in our storage cell but is achievable only when you are fully convinced and has the will to accept change.

It has two fold benefits –

One - you don't need to fight with yourself everyday whenever you are trying to put the new idea in place thinking whether it's the best way to proceed and there is no other conflicting idea which directly opposes the new one thereby saving a lot on time and enhance quality of the processed output.

Two – though our brain has unlimited capacity but it's you who need to take the grind if you have to keep too many things in active mode and use them regularly. So by unlearning certain things which may not be required in near future you generate space for the active mode to operate with minimal things of substance kept their, highly increasing your chances for making a faster and accurate decision which will not only be correct but up to date and modern as well.

Simply because now every time you are using the newer version hence the output quality will improve and since the idea is in active mode already so the processing time will reduce substantially. In this case we don't need to go back and recall anything which was saved in our memory years back and rusting somewhere taking valuable storage space in our brain.

Let's take two quick and modern examples to clear all our doubts…

First one – I had been using *Windows Explorer* for a long time… Suddenly I started noticing that some of the applications are no more working in this and I kept getting reminders to change my system to higher versions available. I ignored thinking who will take the grind and continued with the older version for some time more until I was made redundant and had to take enormous pain one late Friday evening to actually upgrade my system to *Google chrome* and could only rest in peace thereafter. Had I have done it with the first few warnings I may not have wasted so much of my energy and effort and take unnecessary tension during the fag end of this conversion. True I needed time to buy in the new idea and convince myself but shouldn't have taken that long when the writing on the wall was loud and clear.

Today unfortunately I still have the *Internet Explorer* in my system but believe me, I am looking for the first opportunity to unlearn the same and clear off from my hard disk as soon as possible.

In reality it is difficult even to identify what needs to be unlearned and extremely difficult to actually unlearn a thing of past mostly because of the adoptability, bonding and the fear factor associated with it.

Second one –

A related one again – Let facts be told who doesn't have a Desktop or a Laptop for use today? In most certainty all of us have. For personal use we take utmost care whenever we do any financial transaction from these trusted instruments and many a times avoid to do the transactions from our handsets (Mobile phones, tabs etc) purely due to security reasons at least until recently, though the later is more handy and saves time. Time has come when many of the applications are slowly moving to handsets only and soon we will not even be able to download them in your Laptop, forget about using them. True this is a business strategic move and I foresee, that in next couple of years all your transitions may only be possible through handsets only.

Again I got the idea right but just too reluctant at this juncture and still to conceive in my inner soul though that I need to move out from my dear Lappy someday sooner for all my transactions.

Emotions only holds us back and we need to master the art to overcome it if we want to be successful and keep up the pace.

Lets us face the facts that with newer developments and smart phones available to mass now the future of *SMS* looks quite bleak to me as it has lost the purpose since it has many limitations now compared to the modern way of exchanging messages in various advanced forms. Go back a bit in memory and think how closely you held this **sms** (Short Message Service) close to your heart not very long ago and if I would have advised to unlearn the same few years back none would have taken me seriously but I am sure today you will buy in this idea – That's life and we need to proceed further and not look back. True unlearning is not always necessary to learn new things in life but it's essential as we don't intend to overload our brain with junk and obsolete things as they may crisscross with great velocity within us sometimes to hinder our progress in the right direction at the right moment when available time is of great essence and always constant.

To stimulate your brain and keep it in sharp mode here is a simple trick you may use. This is timeless, proven, works wonders and no penny needs to be invested I assure you.

The Kallings theory to sharpen your brain …

Take a pen and a piece of paper, sit calmly and relax for a few moments. Select an eventful date in your life, Say – Your Birthday for example – and now start going down the memory lane slowly. Ask yourself what you did special this last birthday and write a few notes, now think last year what special you did on the same day, last to last year and so on as you go back and back until you remember nothing at all regarding even this most eventful date in your life. As you start going back you will realise that you need to work harder and harder even to write one single sentence and you are still thinking and trying just to write something - what you did on the same day about just a decade back. The ability will of course differ from person to person which is not of much significance if you are ready to develop the habit now. This will help to stimulate the brain and smoothen it to maximum extent without taxing too much and improve its ability to respond sharply in a difficult situation when you try and retrieve old data from it as and when required. This is what keeps the brain agile and like a child as well. Keep this game for your life it does help. You may choose any eventful date as per your liking to play this mental game.

It will never be obsolete for sure in many centuries to come.

Every time you play this game change the event date to bring in more variety and colour as well to your life. This also helps you to identify any commitment you may have given to your near and dear one but missed out and definitely time for retrospection and correction as well. Sometime you may even get emotional as you rewind your memory and discover a younger you much to your likings.

Learning's...

You don't need to hit the gym everyday to keep your body in shape if you are willing to learn a trick or two… Similarly to keep your brain agile, sharp and reap maximum benefit out of it, unlearn to learn new things if the situation demands that. Don't attach an emotional quotient to everything which you are used to for a long time in your life and if the need arises don't hesitate to send it to the bin. If you change you may still lose but if you don't you will soon be in place called dime a dozen…

Time that's exclusively yours

With signs of more and more grueling days ahead, both in professional and personal life it's bound to take its toll if you are not better prepared to fight this demon well in advance and stay focused, cool and composed. Nothing works better than having that refreshing look every morning you sit in your office desk. Is it practically possible? It's achievable if only you have the will to make it happen. One thing is guaranteed – as you get on with your job with every passing day if you are on your upward curve both the pressure and the quantum of job will only go North i.e. increase - making it more and more difficult to find time to relax and keep something exclusively for yourself as time gets distributed to various things and you tend to ignore your basic needs giving it the last priority.

Under such circumstances instead of grumbling and telling the world how over worked you are try to be more efficient in what you do and avoid doing things in a repetitive manner, always look for a more simplified way of completing the task with minimal effort and maximum result. Always conserve your vital energy for the best shot later and keep yourself refreshed. Ability to manage time and fix priorities with perfection shall decide how much you can still keep for yourself. Getting worked up at the drop of a hat, on arrival of a new boss, a new task or change of department doesn't always mean worst is about to follow in fact it often works the opposite way opening doors to new opportunities a plenty.

As you grow up, apart from your professional work your personal engagement in family is bound to increase too. You may no more have time to freak out in the evening with your favourite pack of friends you were so used to before but may look like a forbidden dream now. It's all a part of growing up and completing that life cycle you own with uncertainty at every stage growing by time as you handle more and more so the probability matrix will also ensure that uncertainties visit you at regular interval to keep you engaged and engrossed.

Do you raise your hands and resign to your fate then? Never I suppose, instead you try and find solutions to have a perfect

"Work and life balance."

Work - (Career & Ambition): Life - (Health, Pleasure, Leisure, Family, Friends & Spiritual developments)

True you believe in the above but how to get there? In order to achieve the same you need to reduce your stress many a notches than your present levels. Manage your time in such a way that you still have something left exclusively when you can alone sit in that favourite couch of yours, listen to your best collections or sip in that special drink in complete peace and absolute harmony. When in the world perhaps only you belong and everything else is just secondary. That's life go for it. If you can manage this hour or two in your weekly routine it shall enhance your energy a lot and rejuvenate you to the maximum extent possible working wonders in all spheres of your life.

Difficult and almost impossible to make it a daily routine in your packed schedule for sure but more often you can manage this exclusive time for yourself in a week the more wonders it will bring for you and even enhance your work life to a great extent. Actually our nerves and brain also need rest to recharge and when you perform their favourite activity they get that vital rest and *stimulate to relax mode* there by not only saving their energy for future but also recharging their cells for a high intensity task later which they will perform to perfection.

This stage is not exactly a standby mode you achieve by sleeping or taking complete rest shutting all your activities, rather this is a relax mode where your stimulations of a perfect relax mode matches with that of your brain and body as you tuned them that way hence both go to that desired stage and perfectly coexist with each other in a sequence I denote it as -- "

Cherished Mode."

Our ability to hit this mode more often is like the probability of hitting the *Tee shot* or *Ace* in golf – where you hit the hole in one shot only... but if you try more and more to reach that Cherished mode your cherished dreams will not be further away as well.

Leanings'...

To keep the focus on and release the ever increasing pressure it's important to find a work and life balance and achieve that cherished dream in your life...

Go have a blast

Not very often in your professional career you will get a chance to *"Go have a blast"* for your own achievement. Instead of realising that towards the fag end of your life or career, live in the moment and don't miss the opportunity at that instant to enjoy at your fullest with your best company, be it your family, friends, colleagues or that special someone in your life..

Time runs away at a breath taking speed counting of minutes and hours in your life hardly helps as the intensity of competition is ever increasing so to achieve something worth mentioning may also come very far and in between and you may be already by then engrossed in so many other things that the desired kick may altogether miss from your scheme of things at that juncture.

Have a heart for yourself here and take that vital break to unwind yourself doesn't really matter whether it is for a few hours or a few days, if possible with people who are equally excited in your achievement and who truly loves you. Going out with a wrong company on your best day may be a major mistake which should be avoided. Also remember, on your accomplishment not all visible in your vicinity will be as excited and forth coming so do well to understand this and keep a level head going forward and aware of all those who may ask questions and try their best to put you down at the very first opportunity you provide them. This is bitter truth wherever on earth you live.

The *"Go have a blast"* theory helps in two dimensions in your life.

One – It helps to cement that achievement of yours in various compartments of your body and soul and sends a good positive message to all those who matters in life for you.

Two – Its helps you to live in the moment and do further self introspection and plan where to go from here and so on...

It will definitely energise you to get further motivated and make a real dash towards your ultimate destiny...

Leaning's...

It's difficult and almost impossible to make a major impact everyday in your professional life but as you keep working hard towards it, do not hesitate to enjoy and have fun when the tree is bearing the fruit before this fascinating time runs out and you regret — all your life.

<u>Success</u>

Never let the **Thrust** in you **Dry**

Never let the **Fire** in you **Die**

Never let the **Creativity** in you **Shy**

Never let that **Originality** in you **Lie**

Let the **Passion** in you **Fly**

Let the **Desire** in you **Burn**

Until you **Reach** that **Turn**

Where **Everything** is **Sweet** and **Fun**

We all want to be there **Drenched** in **Sun**

I am not **surprised** if you are the only **One**

Hardly a few will **Reach** there if not **None**

See you there **Soon**… I am all **Done!!!**

Kallings…